Reflections from the Front Porch

poems by

Mike Gill

Finishing Line Press
Georgetown, Kentucky

Reflections from the Front Porch

Copyright © 2022 by Mike Gill
ISBN 978-1-64662-868-1 First Edition
All rights reserved under International and Pan-American Copyright Conventions. No part of this book may be reproduced in any manner whatsoever without written permission from the publisher, except in the case of brief quotations embodied in critical articles and reviews.

ACKNOWLEDGMENTS

"Squirrels Again" was first published in *Buzz-Zine,* vol. 1: Human Animal Relations, edited by Jessica Stokes and Michael Stokes

Publisher: Leah Huete de Maines
Editor: Christen Kincaid
Cover Art: Mike Gill
Author Photo: Mike Gill
Cover Design: Elizabeth Maines McCleavy

Order online: www.finishinglinepress.com
also available on amazon.com

Author inquiries and mail orders:
Finishing Line Press
PO Box 1626
Georgetown, Kentucky 40324
USA

Table of Contents

Milkweed 1

5:15am 2

In Our America 3

Hey, Fox 5

Mint 8

Maple 11

Nickle Deposits 14

4:30 15

They 16

Hate Tastes Like Soap 18

Have You Ever Grown Kkaennip 19

Cicada on the Sage 20

껌딱지/ Sticks Like Gum 21

Squirrels and Cucumber Beetles 22

Phone Calls During a Pandemic 25

Waiting 26

20 Milligrams 27

Squirrels Again 28

Bring Your Own Weather to a Picnic 29

To H and B

"Milkweed"

Do you remember that feeling as a child when you were unsure what would happen when you woke up? The recurring dream where you were swinging on a rope over a canyon. Often you were naked in this dream too. But for some reason, you were never scared, or cold, or excited. But this dream happened all the time. Once a week you would wake up from this dream. Maybe the rope broke, and you were falling. You never hit the ground. What would happen if you did? Is it true that when you die in a dream, your body also stops breathing? Usually you woke up wanting to pee. Or mildly disturbed that you had once again been swinging naked over a canyon holding onto a rope.

Then one day the dreams stopped. No more swinging. Who knows why or how? It is as if the roots were dug up, covered with sourness, and left to bake in the hot sun. Certainly, the feelings of uncertainty did not disappear. No, they remain. The swinging and feeling of being exposed remain. Sometimes you can cover yourself in the curtains or pretend to not see those that stare back, but still there you are waiting for something to happen. With a gust the seeds spread. Perhaps it is fine to let the growth reemerge. You never did hit the bottom.

"5:15am"

Perched on the phone cord, the female cardinal calls out. Every morning, at the same time, she sings. Walking past with my dogs in the time between dark and light, I wonder what does she want? Who is she calling to?

Three years ago, two robins took over a hanging basket at our house to build their nest. We watched with fascination as the flowers died to be replaced by twigs, found cotton, leaves, and other organic material. Four bright blue eggs emerged one day. If we stood on a chair, looked out the window, and hoped the adult robins were off the nest, we could steal a glance at these treasures. We eagerly kept watch hoping for signs of hatching. The four eggs turned into three chicks. Later one of the chicks fell out of the nest and died. Our spring of hope became contextualized as one of grief and loss. When the chicks left the nest, all that was left was an empty nest, dead flowers, and a sense of wondering how these birds will be shaped by their time in the hanging basket. E.J. Koh writes that "privacy is the shadow of grief."[1] Do birds grieve in private? When a fledgling dies, how do those that survive mourn?

Are these robins seeking out answers to where their children went? Apparently only 25 percent of all robins survive the first year, but even with so much death, certainly there has to be some type of mourning, of remembering. Is the cardinal, at the same time each morning calling out to her friends to remember? Is she celebrating living another day? Or eagerly awaiting her death? Humans look to non-humans for answers often reading behavior as signs of something. Is this cardinal missing someone? Is she warning others in the neighborhood of a predator?

The daily 5:15 song remains a mystery. Much like the fledglings, this cardinal will disappear one day.

1 E.J. Koh, The Magical Language of Others (Tin House, 2020): 14.

"In Our America?"

About two weeks after Minneapolis police officer Derek Chauvin murdered George Floyd, yard signs appeared in the neighborhood. These new signs declared that "Black Lives Matter." The signs did not come out during (or after) the murders of Philando Castile, Ahmaud Arbery, or Breonna Taylor. Yet in June 2020, as much of the country was emerging from Covid-19 lockdowns, and activists were calling for police accountability and defunding, these signs started appearing on the front lawns and windows of the houses in my neighborhood. I would walk by these signs with my dogs noticing that they were not appearing in front of the houses where people of color lived. These signs were outside homes where white people lived. Some of these signs were handmade, others were purchased from local organizations, or ordered online. These signs were placed alongside others that had been there for a while, including the Bernie for president, abolish prisons, and the ubiquitous "In Our America" signs.

In our America. 3 short words that contain so much violence and oppression. Our neighborhood full of 1920s and 1930s homes is built on stolen Indigenous land, the ancestral homeland of the Onondaga people, one of the five nations of the Haudenosaunee Confederacy. In our America. In downtown Syracuse is a statue of Columbus. In this representation, the white Italian is standing on four heads of Indigenous individuals. Despite years of activism by Indigenous leaders, the statue remains celebrating white settler colonialism. In our America.

Those yard signs emerged after the presidential election of 2016. Some individuals felt the need to assert that Trump and his supporters' articulation of America was not theirs. The signs declare things like equality among all people, celebration of diversity, that Black lives matter, immigrants and refugees are welcome, that love wins. Disabilities are respected as well, and women are in charge of their bodies. In our America.

Yet, history teaches otherwise. As do the lived experiences of people of color. So do the experiences of trans and gender nonconforming people. Disabled people. Anyone who is not white, straight, able-bodied, what Goffman calls someone without a spoiled identity. Spoiled milk makes you vomit. A spoiled identity does what? In our America.

The United States of America is a nation built upon settler colonialism and forced enslavement. White supremacy is everywhere. In our America. Indeed.

Our. Webster helps out here: of or relating to us or ourselves or ourself especially as possessors or possessor agents or agent, or objects or object of an action.[2] Phew. Our is an ability to claim agency, ownership. Whiteness = our? Other definitions mention belonging or relating to us. In our America. The colonizers reasserting their ownership. Their possession. In our America. I am white. This is not my America. As if.

---

2 "Our." *Merriam-Webster.com Dictionary*, Merriam-Webster, https://www.merriam-webster.com/dictionary/our. Accessed 16 Aug. 2020.

"Hey, Fox"

How does it go? The fox came out on a chilly night. He prayed for the moon to give him light.

I should have known something was up when my dog started barking. Her bark clear and urgent in the early morning. We usually walk up and down the street. I wait for her to pee. She waits for me, or her sister. I want to go back to bed. She wants to explore the neighborhood. It is a battle of wills. She wins. Mostly. This particular morning as her sister was taking her time smelling the remnants of something, across the street I notice something that seems not dog, cat, or deer like. These are the three most common suspects. There might be an occasional skunk, but it's hard to miss their presence. She once scared a raccoon up a tree. But this not dog, cat, or deer like creature was not moving at all.

In fact, it was staring right back at us. The one dog still smelling away. The sister losing her early morning shit barking and making a horrible whining sound. We were quite the sight I am sure. One of us not bothered, one most certainly bothered and me trying to figure out how to respond. Hey, fox. Are you a fox? I think you are. As a kid, my only reference was Maid Marian on the animated Robin Hood. She seemed nice. And cute. I might have had a crush on her. But this fox. They were certainly not cartoonish. Or really interested in hanging out. This fox was checking us out and wondering what our next move was. The one dog stopped smelling and knew something was up. Maybe it was her sisters' whine, or the smell of desperation and nerves now creeping out of my pores.

Are urban foxes good luck? Can you say to your lover, that today will be a good day because you spotted a fox? I was not feeling particularly fortunate that morning. I'm still here, as are my dogs. The fox is still around too. Mischief. Cunningness. Deceptive. Agility. Playfulness. These are some of the many interpretations available for the appearance of a fox in your dream. But we were not dreaming.

When I initially was sharing my tale of the fox encounter, I told others that they were the size of a large dog. That isn't true. This fox is more medium size. Not that it matters. In my mind that morning it was huge. And out to get us. But inside, on the porch, reflecting on our encounter, I realize my assessment of the situation was off. This fox was not out to get us. Perhaps this was the first morning it had decided to hunt on the block, and it was curious what we were. And what we were up to.

There isn't any moral here. No special story. Maybe we will get to encounter each other up close one day. I remember when I lived in Chicago, a coyote walked into a sandwich store. That made news. But my fox meeting only became minor neighborhood gossip. There are pictures of this coyote in front of a soda cooler. It apparently needed to rest. Or was curious. Or wanted a toasted sub sandwich. Maybe the neighborhood fox wants some company. It can get lonely at 5:30 in the morning.

I don't think I will start leaving out food for you fox. But that is a thing in some cities. Oh humans. Evidently, there are too many deer in our city. I'm not sure who gets to say there are too many. The plan for these deer: culling. Which is just a fancy word for murder. The deer in our city are being murdered. Shot. Because apparently, they were contributing to Lyme disease and eating gardens and plants. The lilies and hostas in our garden are often munched by the deer. But kill them for that? Nah. Some other suggestions offered before killing was decided, including giving the deer birth control. Here is some Depo for you all. Wow. Is Deer eugenics a thing?

I found out there is a wide debate too about fox culling/murder. Like deer, apparently death by car is a more effective way to kill foxes. This poem got morbid fast. Why can't it just be a poem about a Maid Marian style fox and my dogs sharing a moment on the street? Life doesn't often reflect animated movies. One day I will realize it has been weeks, or even months without a fox sighting. And I'll momentarily wonder what happened. It is like that though. These encounters leave an impression in the moment but slowly the ridges of that impression fade away. Hey, fox. Be well.

"Mint"

Buzzing, sweetly smelling
Growing tall
Who planted you?
Dogs peeing
Children sniffing
Wasps going in and out

Rain and storms weigh heavy
Bending down to say hello
As July becomes August
It is harder to be tall
No need
You have done well

Next spring you will emerge
I don't know why you picked that corner
Whatever the reason
You chose well
Mint, sweet mint
Grow tall

Maybe you will continue to spread
Your herbal salve for all
Oh mint
Tall mint
I smell you as I pass
Or the wind takes your fragrance into the porch

Monty Don said you spread "voraciously"
That you, mint, can become a weed[3]
I have heard similar advice
But for me there is beauty in your expansion
Grow wide
And tall

3 https://www.montydon.com/tips-and-advice/april Accessed 20 Aug 2020.

Dear mint
Let me go on record
And say I would prefer
You mint
Over the bishop's weed
Growing in the back

It is all about perception
I suppose
I have tried to control the bishop's weed
But it does not yield
To the non-toxic methods
I attempt

Nature is hard to control
Right, mint?
You and your friend the bishop
Grow and grow
One is considered food
The other invasive

The other supposedly unwelcome
Residents of the area
The deer do not eat either
Of you
Maybe if they ate "weeds"
And not "plants"

The settlers would rejoice
But we do not, mint
We toil and mulch
Spray and trap
Shoot and kill
All that gets in the way

The pollinators
Come out to play
When you display
Your white flowers
Letting them dance
About

Dearest mint
Thank you
For allowing us
The opportunity
To be with you
In communion

I don't care what
Others might say
You are a joy
And I will not take
Your appearance for
Granted

Grow mint
Until you are done
I will appreciate
You and stroke
Your sweet leaves
And take in your fragrance

"Maple"

Towering tall
Roots deep
Instant attraction
As a child
We could never afford
Real maple syrup
The Real always capitalized
Imitations are often
Good enough
A fake Picasso
Can be as beautiful
As the original
Yet
There will always
Be someone
That insists
They can tell
The real and the fake

Have you seen that show
Fake or Fortune
Hunting
Sleuthing
Guessing
Is this real
Or not
Indeed, does it matter
Only for the capitalists

I once went to a maple hut
In Eastern Connecticut
I learned that
40 gallons of sap
Is boiled
And boiled

And boiled even more
Into 1 gallon of syrup
Wood, fire, energy
Evaporation
Making sweetness

The angel's share
Is the whiskey that
Evaporates out of
The barrel
Angels like
Single malt
But they are
Not picky
Any whiskey
Or syrup will do
Even if it is imitation

Red maple
Growing tall
Have you ever been
Tapped
Do you share your
Sweet sap
With the angels
The spirits
The squirrels
And foxes

What happens to
Your sap
When it does not
Flow into a bucket
Are there reservoirs
Or sap

Deep below
Even deeper and wider than
The roots you send

Tall maple
Humans have ruined
The world
Cut down your siblings
Your sap
A salve
Nurturing
Strengthening
Flowing out
Deep and wide

"Nickel Deposits"

I grew up in a state where you were not charged bottle deposits. But we would vacation in a neighboring state that charged 5 cents per bottle and can. After a week of playing on the beach, sand in every part of our bodies, my siblings and I would take the empty beer bottles and pop cans to the little grocery store off main street. Three adults and three children drinking various canned drinks for a week would generate almost 3 dollars. With our winnings, for our labor, we bought candy to keep us entertained for the long drive home in the station wagon.

Years later and in a different state, near a college campus known for large parties, the night before garbage collection, individuals are laboring to turn each bottle and can into something more substantial. I'm amazed how hard these individuals work. Walking from bin to bin looking for anything that can be exchanged. 100 cans for 5 dollars. Hours of labor for 25 dollars. Plastic bags are dripping with soda, warm beer, sweet and sticky. Middle class white people looking down. Some are even hostile, violent. This type of labor is not celebrated by liberals or conservatives. I have never once heard of a politician, or pundit celebrate, or express concern for the individuals laboring with cans and bottles.

It is supposedly cute when white children return bottles for candy. But calls of "crime" and "punishment" come forth when the evening bottle collectors emerge. A nickel. The system is rigged when one night of work leaves you only with 25 dollars and a fragrance of alcohol and frat boy desperation. Take what you will from this. Many will regrettably say, but we don't want them going through our trash. Does the privilege of middle-class whiteness extend to the trash can? I can throw away things, but you can't get them. The politics of trash sure are fascinating. There is sarcasm there. The person throwing away the can doesn't seem to want to collect the nickel. But I'll be damned if you can turn my empties into anything.

"4:30"

There is little that can be done
When a 14-year-old
Schnoodle wants her dinner
It's time she barks
Feed me

Way back when
She was fed at 6pm
Now that would be too late
For her and me
Unbearable, perhaps

This granny dog
Loves her treats
Meals
Snacks
Food

Just like me
I get it
But maybe can
We not start the
Feed me ritual too early

Hold tight
I have not yet
Forgotten to feed you
Tonight won't
Be any different

"They"

Each morning, they walk by. Past the mint and flowers on their way somewhere. Inside I am drinking coffee, sitting down to another day in quarantine.

Are you on your way to work? Or to meet your secret love? It is funny how we go about our days. Weeks and months pass and without a notice of those that walk by. Yet, when we are forced inside because of fragile immunity, the window becomes a type of television set. The characters of the neighborhood in a daily drama.

As a kid, my parents were told I was gifted. I'm not entirely sure what that means except I was able to attend a special program once a week. The kids from my school boarded a bus and we all went to this other school, joining all the supposed gifted kids from across the city. Apparently when we all came together, we formed a beautiful mosaic, the various tessera creating something else.

At this program we would imagine other worlds. Medieval banquets. The solar system. Once a week we did feel special. Or at least I did. I would escape my classmates and join others unknown to my siblings, parents, to everyone in my little neighborhood school world. The little fat kid exploring a new realm.

I am reminded of these moments as I sit inside my covered front porch alternating between bites of toast, sips of coffee, and email replies. As you walk by, I make up some story, not based at all in any form of reality, about where you are going. As the months stack up since I have been inside a store, or café, or hugged someone I don't live with, these imaginations get more elaborate.

Yet, I also feel like I am getting more distrusting of those outside my little bubble. I once read a story of a kid that was told she was allergic to the outside world and so had to spend all her life inside.

I'll ruin the story for you. It was all a scam. Her mom was worried she would die like her sibling and father. A weak immunity becomes a plot device. The cute boy that moves next door upsets the entire plan. Love leads to risk.

There is of course one deeply important thing I ought to mention about that gifted program. It was housed in the same building where the kids receiving special education services were located. One group was supposedly gifted, the other disabled. To reinforce this division, some administrator thought it was wise to paint a line dividing the lunchroom. Us on one side, them on the other. As a young kid, the violence of ableism cut deep across the gym.

I tell my students about this experience. How some decision made created a barrier. Little kids that could be friends, any opportunities for love, or hate forbidden. What was not allowed because of that line?

I'm back on the wrong side of that line. Unlike last time, I am here because I think I need to be. I don't want to get sick. And I certainly don't want to infect someone else. So, I sit, here. And you walk by out there.

I'll resist some trite and packaged optimism. From where I sit, few might understand the choices we make. Pay no attention to them. Do what you need to. But as we do so, we understand these lines will separate. My immune system here. Yours there. I'm back in the lunchroom wondering what happens over there.

"Hate Tastes Like Soap"

1985. Your father grabs you
From the kitchen table
Down the hallway
Into the bathroom
Spit and anger from
His lips fall down
He reaches for
The bar of soap
Jams it into your mouth
Soap covering your young teeth
"You do not tell your
Brother You hate him"
He foams
Frightened, you have
Never seen him like this
Decades later you can
Close your eyes
And be transported back
To that violence
Frightened child
You did nothing wrong
Family members joke
About this event
Each time you are
Transported back to
That moment as
Soap mixes with fear
Your father red, angry
Hate fermenting

"Have You Ever Grown Kkaennip"

There is nothing quite so satisfying
As going out to the back deck
And cropping fresh kkaennip
Green like the spring on one side
Deep purple on the other

When I lived in Seoul
In an apartment in the basement
Before *Parasite* made it popular
I could walk outside
And see all my neighbors
Growing the fragrant plant

Urban gardens can be as
Elaborate as an old foam cooler
Kkaennip does not seem to care
If it grows in the ground
Or in a makeshift pot

When the seasons shift
And the birds start nesting
Prepare some dirt
In a sunny area
Sprinkle the tiny seeds
Water and wait

If you are lucky
And Fiacre is near
By mid-June
At the latest
You should be able to enjoy
The minty-herby-earthiness
Of the kkaennip

"Cicada on the Sage"

Your dead body clinging
To the sage
What has life
Been
Years Below
Weeks Above
There is beauty
In your lasting act

껌딱지/ Sticks Like Gum

껌딱지. Pronounced like ggeomddakjji, full of double letter combinations that make the non-fluent stumble. A clunky translation reminds you of the gum stuck to the bottom of your shoe. The kind that has melted on the sidewalk before you step on it, your weight transferring the sticky gum to your sneaker. Once the gum is there it is hard to get off. Even removing the bulk of the gum does not eliminate the residue. You get the idea. With every step you leave a little bit but cannot eliminate the original offender. Even using ice, peanut butter, or an industrial lubricant cannot remove everything.

Have you ever had a 껌딱지? There are many examples online. Clips of the grandfather and the cow. The cow acting like a dog, the two taking a walk. Love and company between the two. The grandpa giving the cow melons as snacks. 껌딱지 come in lots of pairings. Siblings. Dogs. Lovers. One following the other. Yet, despite the name, where one sticks, both benefit. Constant companionship. A deep relationship. Dependence upon the other. Where I go, she follows. Upstairs, downstairs, back porch, or front. Whining if apart.

What happens to the one that survives the pairing? When one dies, how can the surviving partner mourn? If for 6 months, 14 years, or a lifetime, they went everywhere you did and now are no longer there, how do you carry on? The spectral felt in the empty spot on the couch. No longer there. She isn't waking up from her nap to make sure you are nearby. No more searching throughout the house to find you. No more tail wagging when you come home. Somehow the concept does not seem to do justice to the relationship. What starts as one following another becomes more complicated. Not an inconvenience. Or a nuance. But a missing part, made complete in the presence of another. Dear 껌딱지 stick around a bit longer.

"Squirrels and Cucumber Beetles"

While it is still cold outside
You plant seeds in containers
Reusing milk cartons
And egg crates
Nurturing the seedlings
Tomatoes, squash, peppers
Eager for the warmer days
And future harvests
As the little seedlings grow
You prepare their beds
Nutrient rich
Selecting the sunniest spots
Memorial Day passes and your put them in the ground
Grow well
Thanking the earth and spirits

The days lengthen
The seedlings grow
True leaves emerge
As the tomato plant grows tall
You anticipate the sweetness
Building structures
Eager to help them
Little flowers emerge
Followed by tiny green fruit

At that time yellow and black bugs
Appear on the cucumber and squash plants
You take no notice
These must also be pollinators
Bored one morning though
You search and find out
That these visitors
Also want to feast on the cucumber
Taste the green

Supposedly the bitterness of nasturtiums
Ward off these bugs
And you try sprinkling cayenne
On the green tomatoes
To protect them from the squirrels
You have put in many hours
And want to taste summer
Sharing becomes more difficult

You buy neem oil
Prepared to stop the beetles
Spraying once
Then twice
Picking the bugs off the plant
How did they find us
You wonder

The green tomatoes meanwhile
Are growing bigger
You think the squirrels are
Not going to bother them
How naive you are
One morning you wake to find
The largest and greenest tomato
Half-eaten
The remnants on the deck
Taunting you

You remember the old man
That lived across the street
From the school you attended
As a child
He would trap the squirrels
That would go up his trees
Squirrel killer you would all
Taunt him from the playground
Years later for a brief moment
You understand his impulse

Your partner though is the better half
Reminding you that there are plenty
Of fresh tomatoes and cucumbers
To be bought
Let the squirrel have their fun
At least they are leaving
The jalapeno alone

"Phone Calls During a Pandemic"

It is never good
When your father
Calls randomly
On a Tuesday
Morning

During a pandemic
These calls increase
He lets you know
Of another person
That has died

Unable to mourn
Together
These calls
Act like a signal
A sign

You unrealistically
Hope that
By not answering
Death can be
Stopped

"Waiting"

What are you waiting
For

What do you wish will
Happen

It is hard to stay with the
Waiting

The result is the assumed
Reward

Stay for a bit with the
Tension

Welcome the long
Desire

Or greet the uncertain
Dread

"20 Milligrams"

Waking up in the heat
Another long day
Restless
Sitting down
Trying to concentrate
Forcing myself to
Comply
Pretending not
To run away

"Squirrels Again"

Even though you tell yourself it does not matter if the squirrels ruin the garden, you still get upset when they dig up the potatoes. You rearrange the deer netting hoping they will not climb up to the cucumbers. You place the plastic plant trays to protect the growing squash. You sprinkle cayenne. And coffee grounds. This will work you lie to yourself. Surely, they will bother my neighbors, you think. What do they say about magical thinking?

At summer camp, there was a song with the lyrics about chickens and tomatoes. And rabbits and carrots. You don't remember anything about squirrels and vegetables. But there should be something. Even a brief mention that squirrels love to dig up, leave half eaten tomatoes, unripe squash. Taunting the gardener. In a moment of desperation, you bring your tomato plants to your neighbor to foster. She has a supposed squirrel proof enclosure to raise the plants. Seriously, just buy tomatoes at the market next year. Your blood pressure and your neighbor will thank you.

"Bring Your Own Weather to a Picnic"[4]

There is something to be said for living with the certainty that no matter what you face, you can thrive. I envy those that can be so certain that they will not just make it, but when it matters, they can hang in there. Of course, it is totally annoying to be around those with so much self-assuredness. Somewhere deep inside though I am jealous. I wish I had 1/10th of what they have. The ability to face the downpour with conviction that it will not matter. Regardless of the forecast, you pack your sandwiches and head to the park. Sitting inside, peering out, someday might come tomorrow.

---

4 This is a lyric in a song by Lee Sun Hee, "Mama" (2020)

Michael Gill is an associate professor of disability studies in the department of Cultural Foundations of Education at Syracuse University, USA. He is the disability studies minor advisor. Gill is the author of *Allergic Intimacies: Food, Disability, Desire, and Risk* (Fordham University Press 2022) and *Already Doing It: Intellectual Disability and Sexual Agency* (University of Minnesota Press 2015). He co-wrote, with Alexis Boylan, Anna Mae Duane, and Barbara Gurr, *Furious Feminisms: Alternate Routes on Mad Max: Fury Road* (University of Minnesota Press 2020). He also co-edited, with Cathy Schlund-Vials, *Disability, Human Rights, and the Limits of Humanitarianism* (Ashgate 2014). This is his first chapbook.

www.ingramcontent.com/pod-product-compliance
Lightning Source LLC
LaVergne TN
LVHW041508070426
835507LV00012B/1407